Should We Have CAPITAL PUNISHMENT?

JoAnn Bren Guernsey

DISCARD

LERNER PUBLICATIONS COMPANY • MINNEAPOLIS

Library of Congress Cataloging-in-Publication Data

Guernsey, JoAnn Bren
    Should we have capital punishment? / JoAnn Bren Guernsey.
        p.   cm. – (Pro/Con)
    Includes bibliographical references and index.
    Summary: Discusses capital punishment, analyzing how it affects those condemned to die, those who have been victimized, our society, and the enforcers.
    ISBN 0-8225-2602-6
    1. Capital punishment–United States–Juvenile literature. [1. Capital punishment.] I. Title. II. Series: Pro/Con
(Minneapolis, Minn.)
HV8699.U5G84   1991
364.6'6'0973–dc20
                                                    90-21442
                                                        CIP
                                                         AC

Manufactured in the United States of America

1 2 3 4 5 6 98 97 96 95 94 93

CONTENTS

FOREWORD

If a nation expects to be ignorant and free,... it expects what never was and never will be.

Thomas Jefferson

Are you ready to participate in forming the policies of our government? Many issues are very confusing, and it can be difficult to know what to think about them or how to make a decision about them. Sometimes you must gather information about a subject before you can be informed enough to make a decision. Bernard Baruch, a prosperous American financier and an advisor to every president from Woodrow Wilson to Dwight D. Eisenhower, said, "If you can get all the facts, your judgment can be right; if you don't get all the facts, it can't be right."

But gathering information is only one part of the decision-making process. The way you interpret information is influenced by the values you have been taught since infancy–ideas about right and wrong, good and bad. Many of your values are shaped, or at least influenced, by how and where you grow up, by your race, sex, and religion, by how much money your family has. What your parents believe, what they read, and what you read and believe influence your decisions. The values of friends and teachers also affect what you think.

It's always good to listen to the opinions of people around you, but you will often confront contradictory points of view and points of view that are based not on fact, but on myth. John F. Kennedy, the 35th president of the United States, said, "The great enemy of the truth is very often not the lie–deliberate, contrived, and dishonest–

4

but the myth–persistent, persuasive, and unrealistic." Eventually you will have to separate fact from myth and make up your own mind, make your own decisions. Because you are responsible for your decisions, it's important to get as much information as you can. Then your decisions will be the right ones for you.

Making a fair and informed decision can be an exciting process, a chance to examine new ideas and different points of view. You live in a world that changes quickly and sometimes dramatically–a world that offers the opportunity to explore the ever-changing ground between yourself and others. Instead of forming a single, easy, or popular point of view, you might develop a rich and complex vision that offers new alternatives. Explore the many dimensions of an idea. Find kinship among an extensive range of opinions. Only after you've done this should you try to form your own opinions.

After you have formed an opinion about a particular subject, you may believe it is the only right decision. But some people will disagree with you and challenge your beliefs. They are not trying to antagonize you or put you down. They probably believe that they're right as sincerely as you believe you are. Thomas Macaulay, an English historian and author, wrote, "Men are never so likely to settle a question rightly as when they discuss it freely." In a democracy, the free exchange of ideas is not only encouraged, it's vital. Examining and discussing public issues and understanding opposing ideas are desirable and necessary elements of a free nation's ability to govern itself.

This Pro/Con series is designed to explore and examine different points of view on contemporary issues and to help you develop an understanding and appreciation of them. Most importantly, it will help you form your own opinions and make your own honest, informed decisions.

Mary Winget
Series Editor

Paula Cooper, left, was sentenced to death at age 15 for the murder of 78-year-old Ruth Pelke, below.

ONE LIFE
FOR ANOTHER

When Paula Cooper was only 15 years old, she and three other teenage girls from Gary, Indiana, ditched school, started drinking wine and smoking marijuana, and considered ways to get some money to play video games. Ruth Pelke, a 78-year-old Bible teacher, was an easy victim for the girls. They got into her home by saying they wanted to take Bible lessons.

Paula Cooper had brought along a 12-inch butcher knife. She stabbed the old woman 33 times. Mrs. Pelke recited the Lord's Prayer as she died, and the girls made off with $30 for their video games.[1]

The murder outraged members of the community. Despite testimony about her tragic childhood and abusive father, Cooper became the youngest woman in nearly a century to be sentenced to death. Her parents showed no emotion when their daughter was told she would be executed, and they have had little contact with Paula since then.

Paula Cooper spent five of her teenage years on death row. Until she was nearly 20, she spent her days reading and watching TV in a tiny cell at the Indiana Women's

Prison. Sentenced to death in 1986, she was simply marking time while her attorney **appealed** the sentence—in other words, argued in higher courts of law for Cooper's death sentence to be changed to life imprisonment.

Few people in the United States noticed Cooper's birthdays pass and few extended much sympathy toward her. She had admitted to a crime that was startlingly senseless and brutal. And most Americans—almost 80 percent, according to several polls—favor the death penalty for first-degree murder.[2] A Gallup poll released in December 1990, revealed that 77 percent of young people (16 to 24 years old) favor the death penalty.[3]

In other parts of the world, however, Cooper had many supporters. On her 18th birthday, for example, two million Italians signed petitions urging a pardon for Cooper.[4] To those people, she was a symbol of the violence in the United States—violence in the home and on the streets.

Opponents of the death penalty were particularly outraged because she was legally a child—under 18—when she committed her crime. And to some, Cooper, who is black, symbolized racial injustice in the American judicial system. But was she really a symbol or just a dangerous criminal? After all, an innocent victim was killed. Is death by execution an appropriate penalty for murder? This is the most basic question in the debate over capital punishment.

The actions of certain criminals set them apart—even from other criminals. In most U.S. prisons, a special section is set aside to house prisoners who have been sentenced to death (usually for intentional murder) while they wait for their sentences to be either changed or carried out. This section of a prison is commonly called **death row**.

The Rev. Vito Bracone, a Franciscan monk from Italy, traveled to the United States to visit convicted murderer Paula Cooper in the Indiana Women's Prison. Rev. Bracone carried petitions from almost 2 million Italians requesting clemency for Cooper.

As is the case with many death sentences, it was never certain that Cooper would be executed. More than 50 percent of all death sentences in the United States are eventually reversed, and the percentage is even higher in juvenile cases. Also, fewer and fewer juveniles are being sentenced to death.[5]

To Cooper, her years on death row were a nightmare. "I've never really had a chance," she wrote at one point, "and that's all I want."[6]

Many people would argue, "Didn't your victim deserve the same?" Of course. But even Ruth Pelke's grandson pleaded for Paula Cooper's life to be spared—much to the dismay of the rest of the family—and he wrote to her in prison. Why should he care about the girl who murdered his grandmother? Because he believed that it would be just as wrong for the state to kill Cooper as it had been for her to kill Ruth Pelke.[7]

YEARS OF DEBATE

Capital punishment has inspired heated debate for many years, even though the idea seems to have an appealing simplicity. A person has murdered, so he or she must die to even things up—one life for another. Doesn't it make perfect sense? When you add to this the possibility that a death sentence might deter other people from committing similar crimes and the fact that a killer's death prevents him or her from victimizing anyone else, capital punishment seems even more logical.

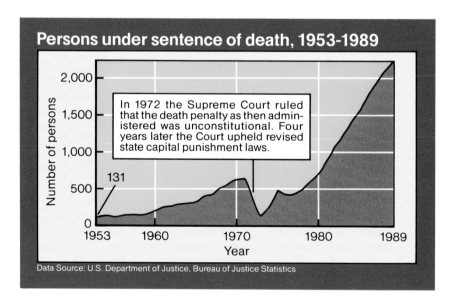

Persons under sentence of death, 1953-1989

In 1972 the Supreme Court ruled that the death penalty as then administered was unconstitutional. Four years later the Court upheld revised state capital punishment laws.

Number of persons

Year

Data Source: U.S. Department of Justice, Bureau of Justice Statistics

When a prisoner is executed, crowds representing both sides of
the capital punishment debate demonstrate outside the prison.

Such views have been widely held throughout history and have determined the punishment for a surprisingly wide variety of crimes—not just for murder. The earliest movement to protest capital punishment in the United States was, in fact, not aimed at actually abolishing the death penalty but at reducing the number of crimes considered to be **capital offenses**—crimes punishable by death. Until the early 1800s, crimes such as robbery, burglary, rape, and arson were punishable by death in many states.[8]

Between 1930 and 1967, according to the U.S. Department of Justice, 3,859 executions were carried out in the United States. In 1935, the peak year, 199 people were executed, but then the numbers began to decline rapidly.[9]

By 1967 those in favor of abolishing capital punishment had become so vocal and powerful that executions came to a complete halt. Lawyers who opposed the death penalty had successfully challenged specific death sentences in various state and federal courts. On the basis of these individual cases, the U.S. Supreme Court decided that the death penalty was **unconstitutional.** With the 1972 decision in *Furman v. Georgia,* the Court held that the death penalty violated the Eighth Amendment, which protects people from "cruel and unusual punishment," and the Fourteenth Amendment, which guarantees "equal protection of the laws." This decision assumes that if a punishment is objectionable because it is *unusual,* it is probably unequal also. The justices, in their five-to-four decision, were far from agreeing as to why they opposed or supported the death penalty. Also, the Court refused to nullify the death penalty—to make it illegal. The Court left open the possibility that the death penalty might be constitutional if imposed for certain crimes and applied uniformly.

Although the Court's decision did not rule out the death penalty, it did bring about a 10-year **moratorium,** or temporary ban, on gassings, hangings, shootings, and electrocutions. (Injections were not yet being used to execute people.) Prisoners were still sentenced to death, but the sentences were not carried out.

On July 2, 1976, however, the Supreme Court ruled, in a seven-to-two decision, that the death penalty *is* constitutional. In *Gregg v. Georgia,* the Court stressed that "the infliction of death as a punishment for murder is not without justification and . . . is not unconstitutionally severe." Shortly thereafter the moratorium came to an end. In January 1977, Gary Gilmore, a self-confessed murderer who argued for his *right* to be put to death, was shot by a firing squad in Utah. His execution was a turning point, and other executions followed. At the time, several hundred people were on death row while they waited for the results of their appeals. Because of the confusion about the legal and moral questions surrounding capital punishment, some of these inmates are still waiting.[10]

EXECUTIONS ON THE RISE

The number of executions has increased recently. On June 14, 1988, a Louisiana prisoner named Edward Byrne became the 100th inmate to be executed since the moratorium was lifted in 1977.[11] During the following three years, more than 50 executions took place. Usually, when someone is executed, a crowd gathers outside the prison walls. The people in the crowd are sharply divided. Some protest the execution of the prisoner while others celebrate the administration of justice. Each group thinks its position is the right one.

As of 1991, the population on death row was approaching 2,500. Thirty-six states have made executions legal again, although fewer than half of these states have carried out any death sentences since the moratorium ended.[12] Currently an average of 300 prisoners are sentenced to death each year, but fewer than 20 are actually executed.[13] This situation has caused an almost impossible backlog of executions on death row. At 10 executions a week, it would take more than four years to kill all death-row inmates—assuming no more were added.

The reason inmates accumulate on death row is that, like all citizens, they have the right to appeal their cases from the lower courts, where cases are first tried, through several higher courts at the state and federal levels. There are many reasons that a case might be appealed. Perhaps the method of arrest violated the accused person's rights. Perhaps the

In 1977 Gary Gilmore, far right, *argued for his right to be executed.*

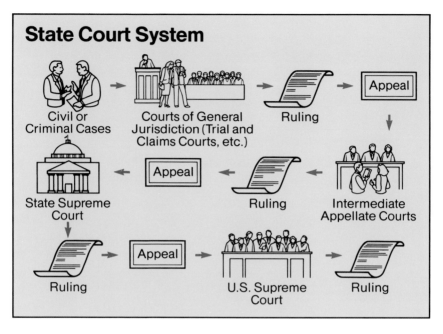

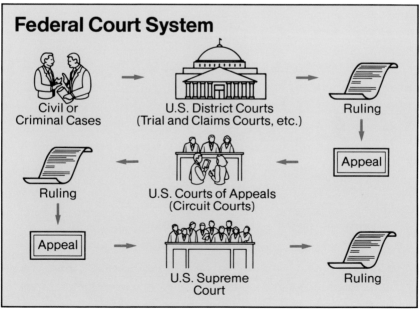

trial was unfair in some way. Or maybe additional evidence surfaced, proving the innocence of the accused person. A ruling can be overturned at any step in the judicial process, so it takes a long time for a decision to become final.

The U.S. Supreme Court is the final step in the appeals process, but its rulings since 1977 have only further complicated the debate. The job of the Supreme Court justices in this matter is not an easy one. The Constitution does not allow "cruel and unusual punishment." But under what circumstances, if any, is execution *not* cruel and unusual?

The Supreme Court saved Paula Cooper's life by ruling that it was unconstitutional to execute anyone who was 15 or younger when he or she committed a capital offense. Cooper has become a model prisoner, getting an education in prison and working to help other young people who are as troubled as she once was. But because of her prison sentence, she could remain locked up until she is 45 years old.[14]

OTHER COMPLEX QUESTIONS

In addition to constitutional interpretation, many other questions enter the debate about capital punishment. The main question always seems to be: Does killing a murderer really make up for the death of the victim? To the victim's loved ones, who are relieved when the ordeal is over and the murderer is dead, the answer is likely to be, "No, but it's all we can get. It's fair."

Does the death penalty send a message that it is okay to counter violence with more violence? Death-penalty supporters see few alternatives. Sentences of so-called life imprisonment have become shorter and shorter. **Parole**, or early release, for even the most dangerous criminal is not

Percentage of those under sentence of death who were executed, by race, 1977-1989

Race	Total under sentence of death, 1977-1989[a]	Prisoners executed	
		Number	% of total
All races[b]	3,746	120	3.2%
White	2,161	71	3.3
Black	1,534	49	3.2

[a] Includes those under sentence of death at the beginning of 1977 (420) plus all new admissions under sentence of death between 1977 and 1989 (3,326).

[b] Includes whites, blacks, and persons classified as members of other races.

Data Source: U.S. Department of Justice, Bureau of Justice Statistics

only possible but frequent. And sentences of life imprisonment without any possibility of parole are seen as burdens on already dramatically overcrowded prisons, as well as on taxpayers. The TV Paula Cooper watches, the books she reads, the bed she sleeps on, the clothes she wears, and the food she eats are paid for by taxes.

IS IT FAIR AND EQUAL?

Questions of fairness and equality in sentencing are among the most troubling in the capital-punishment debate. In addition to the possibility of executing innocent people or people who have truly been rehabilitated, what about racial bias? Does the race of the killer influence, or even determine, his or her sentence? Does the *victim's* race also play a role? The death penalty also raises many other questions—questions with no easy answers.

A LIVING DEATH

*Life on the Row is a blending of the real and the unreal;
it's a clash of internal and external tension, the tension
of everyday living magnified a hundred times. You're a
prisoner in a strange land. You are and you aren't a part
of the larger whole around you. You form friendships
and your friends die. You dream and your dreams die.*
—Caryl Chessman
*Former death row prisoner
San Quentin Prison
Executed May 2, 1960*[1]

Some prisons are undergoing much-needed reforms, but
death row has always been a bleak and highly restrictive
place, isolated from the rest of the prison community as
well as from the outside world.

To get to death row, a visitor must usually pass through
several locked doors or gates, and the impression is often
one of descending more and more deeply into a tomb.
Inmates on death row are usually shut off from natural light
and air. Even prison guards are relieved to escape this
atmosphere each day.[2]

Prisoners on death row spend nearly 24 hours a day in
their tiny cells, alone. Contact with other inmates usually
occurs only through the bars that surround them, and contact with other human beings is always through some kind

of barrier, such as glass. When they leave their cells, the inmates are searched and then chained and cuffed. They are given no work to do and the hours pass slowly.

Death-row prisoners often describe their existence as less than human—mechanical, even "zombielike." They are faced with empty days and continual feelings of being powerless and fearful of the future.[3] And the lengthy appeals process usually takes 6 to 10 years.

Joseph Giarratano, a former death-row inmate in Virginia, described his daily struggle to retain some thread of hope:

> Hope is such a frail thing when hopelessness constantly bombards the senses. You can hear its empty sound in the clanging of the steel doors, in the rattle of chains, in the body searches, in the lack of privacy, in the night sounds of death row, and you can see it in the eyes of the guards who never really look at you, but are always watching to see that you do not commit suicide. You can feel the hopelessness each time you are asked to state your number, when you are holding the hand of a friend in chains who is being pulled away from you, never to be seen again. You can hear it in the echo of a system where humanity is constantly denied. . . . [H]ere on the row, where life goes on, death is never distant. Here life and death are one.[4]

The uncertainties of such an existence make it extremely difficult. Each day, inmates wonder whether or not their latest appeal will allow them to face life imprisonment instead of death. Or, if prisoners claim to be innocent, they wait for the day when they will be believed.*

Many death-row inmates have been abandoned by family and friends. Their connection to the outside world is through their attorneys, and their only hope lies in the legal system.

*Roger Coleman claimed he was innocent until he was executed on May 20, 1992.

A game of checkers on death row

The majority of prisoners on death row, however, are too poor to pay private attorneys. Their legal help has been appointed by the state. But state-appointed attorneys are often overworked, underpaid, and not as well supported by a paid staff as the prosecuting attorneys. A few defense lawyers, such as one who used a racial slur when referring to his client in front of the jury, actually seem incompetent.[5] Other court-appointed defense attorneys, however, have devoted as much as 2,000 hours to a case, spending large sums of their own money on appeals.[6]

Inmates who have not been abandoned experience the additional agony of watching their families and friends suffer. It is only natural to sympathize with, and lend support to, the families of victims. But a criminal's family is likely to suffer tremendous pain as well. The family may spend years battling to save a loved one only to face his or her execution in the end. A criminal's family might also experience humiliation and a sense of guilt.

Under the conditions on death row, human beings almost inevitably change. Some changes are quite positive. Those who had been addicted to drugs or alcohol become free of controlled substances, sometimes for the first time since childhood. Giarratano, the Virginia inmate quoted earlier, is a good example—he is no longer the drug-addicted person he was when he was arrested.

In addition, he and some other inmates have learned to cope, even to blossom in their own ways, during all the hours of solitary contemplation. They may read everything they can get their hands on, including law books to help them advance their own cases or those of friends in neighboring cells. Sometimes all it takes to survive is a preoccupation with the details and routines of their lives— with exercise, food, or mail.

More typically, however, condemned prisoners change in far less constructive ways. They give up eventually and allow themselves to deteriorate both physically and mentally. A few death-row prisoners sink into a private, psychotic world from which there is little chance of their return.[7]

WHO LIVES ON DEATH ROW?

Most recent executions have occurred in southern states. Alabama, Florida, Georgia, Louisiana, and Texas have carried out about three-fourths of all executions since 1976.[8] Florida, Texas, California, Georgia, and Illinois have the largest death-row populations, accounting for about half of all prisoners awaiting execution.[9]

Who lives on death row? According to statistics compiled by the U.S. Department of Justice at the end of 1989, almost all of the 2,250 inmates then awaiting execution were men. Only 25 women were on death row. Fifty-eight percent of the prisoners were white and 40 percent were black. This is a much higher proportion of black men than in the general U.S. population, in which approximately 11 percent are black. The average condemned prisoner was a single male in his early thirties who had not graduated from high school. He also had a history of prior **felony** convictions before he was sentenced to death for committing murder.[10]

In the past, extremely violent offenders were commonly portrayed as monsters or maniacs, incapable of remorse. This "mad dog" stereotype made the death penalty easier to support.

Although there are some prisoners on death row who would fit this description, many others do not. In any discussion of capital punishment, it is important to resist dehumanizing condemned killers. As Stephen Gettinger points out in his book *Sentenced to Die*, "It would be nice if we could get rid of evil by defining it out of the human species, declaring that anyone who does these horrible things is not human. But it will not work. The capacity of man to do evil, no less than good, is what defines us as human."[11]

How did the inmates on death row get there? Many different paths can lead to death row, but the usual route includes repeated failures, blocked opportunities, squashed hopes, and broken dreams. Extreme poverty and child abuse or neglect are often cited as factors leading to violent crime.

Criminal behavior is one way in which some people respond to their seemingly hopeless lives. While many individuals survive a harsh environment without resorting to violence—especially those with strong, nurturing families— others do not adapt so well.

MISTAKES CAN BE MADE

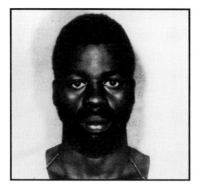

Ronald Monroe

One of the strongest arguments against capital punishment is that, inevitably, someone will die who is innocent. Nobody knows for sure how often this has happened, but many death penalty opponents point to a few men and women on death row who claim to be innocent. Ronald Monroe is one example.

In Louisiana one night in 1977, Monroe was pulled out of bed by police and forced to look at the bloody scene of a neighbor's murder. Lenora Collins had been stabbed in front of her two children, ages 11 and 12, and the children claimed Monroe was the killer. The youngest of 13 children and diagnosed as borderline retarded, Monroe had had no history of violence.

No physical evidence pointed to Monroe's guilt, only the eyewitnesses' stories. Several crucial pieces of evidence in Monroe's favor, including an apparent confession to the Collins murder by a man arrested for another murder, were not presented during Monroe's trial. Sloppy police work and questionable procedures on the part of Monroe's state-appointed lawyers have raised serious doubts about his conviction.

For 13 years after the murder, Monroe's chances for successful appeal have dwindled. While still waiting for his execution date to be set, Monroe has decided on the last words he'll speak as he is strapped into the electric chair: "I'm innocent."[12]

NO EXCEPTIONS?

Can you imagine a young boy in an electric chair, the adult-size straps barely holding him in place? George Stinney, who was executed in 1944 in South Carolina, was 14 years old at the time.[1] In the United States, 281 people under age 18 have been executed.

You might suppose that these executions happened a long time ago, but as of 1989, 31 individuals were on death row for crimes they committed as juveniles.[2] As recently as 1986, South Carolina executed a man who had killed someone when he was 17.[3]

In most of the world, even in countries with such harsh legal environments as Iraq, Libya, and South Africa, the death penalty is not imposed on people under 18. In the United States, the question of imposing the death sentence for a murder committed by someone 16 to 18 years old is left to the states.[4]

One of the reasons capital punishment has become such an important issue recently is the rise in the crime rate among young people. According to FBI statistics, the number of juveniles arrested for murder climbed from 1,311 in 1985 to 2,208 in 1989.[5]

Minimum age authorized for capital punishment, by state, year end 1989

Age less than 18	Age 18	No age specified
Arkansas (15)	California	Alabama
Georgia (17)	Colorado	Arizona
Indiana (16)	Connecticut	Delaware
Kentucky (16)	Illinois	Florida
Louisiana (16)	Maryland	Idaho
Mississippi (13)[a]	New Jersey	Nebraska[b]
Missouri (14)	New Mexico	Pennsylvania
Montana[c]	Ohio	South Carolina
Nevada (16)	Oregon	Washington
New Hampshire (17)	Tennessee	
North Carolina[d]	Federal system[e]	
Oklahoma (16)		
South Dakota[f]		
Texas (17)		
Utah (14)		
Virginia (15)		
Wyoming (16)		

Note: Ages at the time of the capital offense were indicated by the offices of the state attorneys general. Unlisted states do not allow capital punishment.

[a] Minimum age defined by statute is 13, but effective age is 16 based on an interpretation of the U.S. Supreme Court decisions by the attorney general's office.

[b] Age can be a statutory mitigating factor.

[c] Youths as young as 12 may be tried as adults, but age less than 18 is a mitigating factor.

[d] Age required is 17 unless the murderer was incarcerated for murder when a subsequent murder occurred; then, the age may be 14.

[e] Age 18; less than 18 but not younger than 14 if waived from juvenile court.

[f] Age 10, but only after a transfer hearing to try a juvenile as an adult.

Data Source: U.S. Department of Justice, Bureau of Justice Statistics

In his book *Kids Who Kill*, Dr. Charles Patrick Ewing predicts, "We're about to see an epidemic of juvenile **homicide** such as Americans have never witnessed." If the current trend continues, Dr. Ewing says, killings by children could triple or even quadruple by the end of the 1990s.[6]

Why is this happening? Most experts point to factors such as child abuse, extreme poverty and hopelessness, severe psychiatric and brain disorders, and drug and alcohol abuse. In many cities, the population of teenage gangs is increasing, and the gangs are becoming more and more violent. The ready availability of guns is cited as another factor contributing to homicides by juveniles, as is increased exposure to violence on television and in movies. It seems that many young people are becoming **desensitized** to violence. Witnessing murder over and over on a TV or movie screen makes it seem almost routine, and since the killing on TV and in the movies is fictional, the consequences do not appear real either. In many urban areas, children experience real violence on a daily basis as well.

Most murder victims of juveniles are acquaintances, and about 15 to 20 percent of the victims are the juveniles' parents. In many cases, children kill to protect themselves from parental abuse they have suffered for many years.[7]

One example is 16-year-old Richard Jahnke, Jr. From a dark corner of his garage one night in November 1982, as his parents' car pulled into the driveway, Richard shot his father with a shotgun. Because of evidence of long-term abuse at the hands of his father, Richard was convicted of **manslaughter**, a less serious crime than murder.

But not all young people kill in self-defense. In Dr. Ewing's private practice, he sees many children who have an

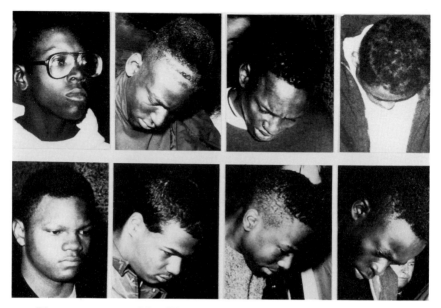

These teens, ages 14 to 17, were charged with beating and raping a female jogger in New York's Central Park in April 1989. The jogger's face and skull were crushed, she lost most of her blood, and she was left for dead.

"antisocial personality disorder." In other words, they lack a conscience. They have what Ewing calls an "almost total lack of regard for human life."[8] This disorder is usually, though not always, associated with severe child abuse.

Because of increased juvenile crime, more and more juvenile offenders are being viewed as vicious predators, "lost" forever. For such individuals, parole would simply give them the opportunity to kill again as adults—adults who have been hardened by prison life. One prominent defender of death-row inmates accuses society of having "totally given up on the idea of reform or rehabilitation for the very young. We are basically saying we will throw those kids away."[9]

A current movement toward harsher penalties for juveniles is, in part, a response to the increase in the number and violence of their criminal offenses. And the Supreme Court, since losing its most outspoken opponent of the death penalty, William Brennan, will be reexamining the minimum age for executing murderers as individual cases are brought before it.

Death-penalty opponents ask that, instead of increasing penalties for the young, we work harder to solve the social problems that contribute to violence. Brutalized children often become brutal themselves, regardless of what punishment is being threatened.

WHAT ABOUT THE MENTALLY IMPAIRED?
Aside from juvenile offenders, are there also people who simply do not understand what they're doing when they commit a murder? In 1986 James Terry Roach was executed

Former U.S. Supreme Court Justice William J. Brennan, Jr., opposed the death penalty.

James Terry Roach, convicted of killing three people in 1977, was 17 years old at the time of the murders. He was slightly retarded and may have had a brain disorder.

in South Carolina for raping and murdering two young women and killing a young man. In addition to being only 17 at the time of the murders, Roach was mildly retarded and may have been suffering from a brain disorder.

As many as 30 percent of the 2,300 prisoners on death row may be retarded or mentally impaired.[10] In 1979 Johnny Paul Penry raped a Texas woman and stabbed her to death. He was 22 years old at the time, but with a mental age of 7. Should he be held responsible for his crime? Should he be put to death for it?

The U.S. Supreme Court heard Penry's case in 1989 and ruled that the constitutional ban on "cruel and unusual punishment" does not automatically forbid death sentences for the retarded. In other words, someone like Penry can be executed.

When asked in nationwide polls, most people strongly disapproved of executing retarded criminals. But it is difficult to measure a person's capacity for judging matters of right and wrong. And it is just as difficult for juries to decide what role a criminal's mental state played in his or her crime.

Demographic profile of prisoners under sentence of death, 1989

Characteristic	Year end 1989	1989 admissions
Total number under sentence of death	2,250	250

Sex
  Male
  Female
	98.9%
	1.1
		97.6%
		2.4

Race
  White
  Black
  Other
	58.2%
	40.1
	1.6
		53.2%
		45.2
		1.6

Ethnicity
  Hispanic
  Non-hispanic
	6.9%
	93.1
		8.4%
		91.6

Age
  Younger than 20
  20-24
  25-29
  30-34
  35-39
  40-54
  55 or older
 	
  Median age
	0.3%
	8.5
	21.6
	26.4
	17.5
	23.2
	2.5
	
	33.6 years
		2.0%
		23.2
		27.6
		21.6
		10.0
		13.6
		2.0
		
		28.6 years

Education
  7th grade or less
  8th
  9th-11th
  12th
  Any college
 	
  Median education
	9.2%
	9.0
	37.2
	35.0
	9.7
	
	11th grade
		9.6%
		5.6
		43.9
		31.8
		9.1
		
		11th grade

Marital status
  Married
  Divorced/separated
  Widowed
  Never married
	29.1%
	23.2
	2.1
	45.6
		23.5%
		19.7
		3.3
		53.5

Data Source: U.S. Department of Justice, Bureau of Justice Statistics

THE SYSTEM

From the point of view of many inmates, the judicial system is not only unfair at times, but seems to trap them in a nearly endless maze of appeals and paperwork, of soaring ups and devastating downs. Imagine having only a few hours left before being executed, then getting a **stay of execution** and being sent back to death row with what seems to be a promise of life, only to return later to face death again. Will it happen this time or not?

Since it takes an average of eight years from the time a prisoner is sentenced to death to the time the execution takes place, many people feel the waiting and the uncertainty are almost worse than the death penalty itself.[12] A few inmates, like Gary Gilmore, have actually *chosen* death over this agonizing fight against it.

In 1991 the U.S. Congress prepared an anticrime bill, which included changes in how death-penalty appeals are handled in the federal courts. Several Republican senators and President George Bush wanted stricter limits on death-row appeals than those contained in the bill. After the president threatened to veto the bill, Congress abandoned the hope of passing it. The chief justice of the U.S. Supreme Court, William Rehnquist, is a powerful ally in the effort to limit the appeals process. Rehnquist told a group of lawyers that the system for handling death-penalty appeals "verges on the chaotic" and "cries out for reform."[13]

Is the problem of capital punishment best solved by limiting the number of appeals a person can make and the number of years during which appeals can be made? Or would this kind of reform mean that more innocent or rehabilitated people would die? As the debate continues, the number of inmates on "the row" continues to climb.

What about those people who were adults and mentally competent at the time of their crimes, but have since changed demonstrably, have shown remorse, and could lead productive lives? Many experts question whether **rehabilitation** can occur within the limitations of a prison system, especially that of death row. But others point to startling examples of criminals, especially young ones like Paula Cooper, who have turned their lives around.

Joseph Giarratano is perhaps the death-row inmate most often pointed to as proof that rehabilitation is possible. His childhood does not distinguish him from other capital offenders. He had an abusive mother and an absent father, he dropped out of school, and he was a drug abuser. In 1979 he turned himself in to police and confessed to the murders of two women. At the time of the murders, he was in a drug-induced psychosis, and he does not actually remember committing the crimes.

His trial took only half a day, and his requests to introduce new evidence that could prove his innocence have been turned down repeatedly. At age 33, he had spent 11 years on death row. During those years, he became entirely drug-free, he educated himself, primarily about the law, and he became an effective **advocate** of other inmates.

Whether he is guilty or innocent, Giarratano certainly is not the same person he was in 1979. In fact, friends and supporters from all over the world have worked frantically to save this man, who, they claim, is a brilliant, sensitive, and extraordinary human being.[11] Giarratano's spirit remained unbroken. Early in 1991, his death sentence was commuted, or changed, to life imprisonment by Governor Douglas Wilder of Virginia. Giarratano could be paroled in 2004.

Ronald Woomer, top left, was executed in April 1990 for the murders of four people.

JUSTICE
OR REVENGE?

In December 1984, Robert Lee Willie, sentenced to death for raping and murdering an 18-year-old woman, was executed in a Louisiana state prison. He issued a statement several minutes before his death: "Killing people is wrong. . . . It makes no difference whether it's citizens, countries, or governments. Killing is wrong."

Two weeks later in South Carolina, Joseph Carl Shaw, an admitted killer about to be executed, made a similar statement about the immorality of killing, no matter who does it. Shaw committed at least three murders and admitted to having mutilated the body of a 14-year-old girl.

Many people find it outrageous when murderers facing the death sentence lecture the public about morality. Is it possible to compare cold-blooded murder to a legal execution?

Edward Koch, former mayor of New York City, wrote a persuasive essay for the *New Republic* magazine. He said:

> Life is indeed precious, and I believe the death penalty helps to affirm this fact. Had the death penalty been a real possibility in the minds of these murderers, they might well have stayed their hand. They might have shown moral awareness before their victims died, and not after. Consider the tragic death of Rosa Velez, who

happened to be home when a man named Luis Vera burglarized her apartment in Brooklyn. "Yeah, I shot her," Vera admitted. "She knew me, and I knew I wouldn't go to the chair."

Koch firmly believes that if people stop tolerating crime, crime will decrease.[1]

MURDER IN THE UNITED STATES

It is true that no other major democracy uses the death penalty. But other countries in the world are not faced with the murder rate that exists in the United States. A murder occurs about every 24 minutes in the United States, a rate that is 4 times higher than Canada's, 8 times higher than Germany's, and 10 times higher than Japan's.[2]

In the United States, the murder rate climbed 122 percent between 1963 and 1980. During that same period, the murder rate in many large U.S. cities increased by 400

Edward Koch, former mayor of New York, supports the death penalty.

Convicted killers John LeVasseur, left, and Gregory Frye, right, play cards on death row. The secured area behind them is a guard post.

percent or more.[3] Perhaps if other countries experienced as many murders as the United States, their citizens might demand harsher penalties as well.

In one New Jersey case, a man named Richard Biegenwald served only 18 years in prison for murder. After his release, he was arrested again and convicted of killing four more people. This kind of repeat offender is not unusual. In New York City, 85 persons arrested for homicide in 1976 and 1977 had previously been arrested for murder.

Even if murderers are kept in prison "for life," this does not necessarily keep them from killing. A prisoner named Lemuel Smith was serving four life sentences for murder (plus two life sentences for kidnapping and robbery) in New York's Green Haven Prison. (In New York, there is no death penalty.) While imprisoned, however, Smith managed

Criminal-history profile of prisoners under sentence of death, by race, 1989

| | Prisoners under sentence of death | | | | | |
| | Number | | | Percent[a] | | |
	All races[b]	Black	White	All races	Black	White
Prior felony conviction history						
Yes	1,456	823	615	69.3	67.0	73.4
No	645	405	223	30.7	33.0	26.6
Not reported	149	82	65			
Prior homicide conviction history						
Yes	180	97	78	9.2	8.5	9.9
No	1,780	1,043	709	90.8	91.5	90.1
Not reported	290	170	116			
Legal status at time of capital offense						
Charges pending	130	80	45	6.7	7.0	5.8
Probation	142	92	48	7.3	8.1	6.2
Parole	410	200	207	21.0	17.5	26.6
Prison escape	36	23	12	1.8	2.0	1.5
Prison inmate	59	39	20	3.0	3.4	2.6
Other status	26	15	10	1.3	1.3	1.3
None	1,148	691	435	58.8	60.6	56.0
Not reported	299	170	126			
Median time elapsed since imposition of death sentence (months)	51	49	54			

[a]Percents are based on those offenders for whom data were reported.
[b]Includes whites, blacks, and persons classified as members of other races.

Data Source: U.S. Department of Justice, Bureau of Justice Statistics

to strangle a female corrections officer and dismember her body.[4] What difference would another life sentence make for this man?

To many people, lessening the penalty for murder shows a low regard for the value of the victim's life. The increased protection of the guilty seems an improper exchange for innocent lives. As Mayor Koch sees it, "It is by exacting the highest penalty for the taking of human life that we affirm the highest value of human life."[5]

But isn't life imprisonment actually worse than death, at least in many cases? Apparently not. The overwhelming majority of inmates make every effort to stay alive. Studies show that 99.9 percent of murderers prefer life imprisonment to death.[6]

ATTEMPTED MURDER

One question that troubles many people is what to do with a criminal who has attempted murder. A person who sets out to kill others, terrorizes, tortures, and almost kills them is usually given a lighter sentence than a robber who kills when confronted by a store owner with a gun. In several cases, armed robbers have been executed even when the murders they committed were not clearly "cold-blooded" or premeditated—planned ahead of time.

The definition of attempted murder can be further blurred by other circumstances. In a recent case in New York, three teenagers were accused of raping and brutally beating a female jogger in Central Park. The jury agonized for hours about how to categorize the actions of the accused. Yes, they

A group of joggers and wheelchair athletes pause for a moment of silence at the spot where a female jogger was raped, beaten, and left for dead in Central Park in New York.

had beaten the victim repeatedly with weapons until her face and skull were smashed. Yes, they had left her for dead, and she had lost nearly all of her blood. In spite of this, she lived, although with permanent damage.

Did her attackers know what it would take to kill someone? The jury, deciding that the accused persons were juveniles and did *not* have such knowledge, found them innocent of attempted murder. Their sentences (for rape and assault rather than attempted murder) were 5 to 10 years maximum—much shorter than if the youths had been convicted of attempted murder.

A LIFE FOR A LIFE?

Another issue in the debate over capital punishment is the question of **restitution**, paying for the crime committed. Is the murderer's death enough, in itself, to make up for the killing of another person? Shouldn't there be some way to deal more effectively with the surviving friends and relatives of the murder victim? If less public money were spent on the appeals process for convicted criminals, wouldn't there be more money to help victims of violent crime and to establish programs to help prevent similar crimes in the future?

By far the most radical approach to restitution has been suggested by Dr. Jack Kevorkian, a pathologist in Royal Oak, Michigan. For nearly 30 years, he has tried to make practical use of the bodies of executed criminals. He suggests harvesting the criminals' organs—hearts and kidneys, for example—to save other peoples' lives. There are never enough organs available for all the people who need them for transplants. And, says Kevorkian, "these men [executed criminals] owe society a debt."[7]

JUSTICE OR REVENGE?

In addition to the question of justice is the related notion of revenge. What is the difference?

Wanting revenge, or vengeance, means wanting someone to suffer because he or she has made another suffer. A person can want revenge even when nothing legally wrong has been done. For example, one girl might want to "get back" at another for beating her in a race.

Some people feel a special kind of satisfaction when a person who has done wrong is made to suffer. The original act has been avenged, and the avenger feels better because of this; the wrongdoer has gotten "what's coming" to him or her. Although the New Testament seems to emphasize forgiveness, the justice of revenge is expressed clearly in the Old Testament: "And if any mischief follow, then thou shalt give life for life, eye for eye, tooth for tooth, hand for hand. . . ."

It is certainly understandable that the loved ones of murder victims would seek the satisfaction, as imperfect as it is, of revenge. It can be agony for the victimized families to know that the person who destroyed their lives will probably live on for years and may even be set free eventually. At the very least, an executed prisoner poses no further threat.

What other legal options do victimized people have? Taking justice into their own hands would result in their own arrests. Execution is often seen as the only punishment that can allow the victim's survivors to go on with their lives. They will always miss their loved ones, but if the murderer is put to death, that can provide at least some sense of justice.

The families of Ronald Woomer's victims, top, await his execution on April 27, 1990. Mrs. Harold Piest, bottom left, the mother of a John Wayne Gacy victim, is escorted to the Chicago courtroom, where the jury unanimously decided on the death penalty.

FAMILIES
OF VICTIMS—
A "LIFE SENTENCE"

It's so damn hard. It's the first thing you think of in the morning and the last thing you think of at night. . . . I think they should have done the same thing he did to the boys—torture him to death. . . . It would make us feel better if he were executed. . . . I can still see his eyes. I know he doesn't have any remorse.
—Norma Nelson about her son's accused killer, John Wayne Gacy
How come he's still living? It would help that justice was done. It's my impression that he's just sort of laughing.
—Robert Nelson, also about Gacy[1]

Robert and Norma Nelson of Cloquet, Minnesota, remember only too vividly the 1980 trial of John Wayne Gacy, Jr., the worst **serial killer** in U.S. history. Their son was one of Gacy's 33 victims. The Nelsons sat with families of other victims (enough to fill several rows in the Chicago courtroom) and watched Gacy's long trial culminate in a death sentence. But that did not end their suffering. In many ways, it was only the beginning.

Ten years later, Gacy was still on death row in Illinois. His appeals were dragging on, in part because he had written 20,000 pages of legal arguments, including **briefs** presented to and rejected by the Illinois Supreme Court. Meanwhile, he was passing the time by painting pictures of clowns and other figures and using his notoriety to sell them.

Gacy, a stocky, 48-year-old man, had worked as a contractor but also entertained children at parties, dressing up as a clown and doing tricks for them. It was difficult for people who knew him then to believe that over the years he had murdered more people than anyone else in the nation. But on the day he was arrested, Gacy confessed to the killings, telling a friend, "I've been a bad boy . . . I killed 30 people, give or take a few."

Twenty-nine of his victims were found buried in the crawl space of his suburban Chicago house, where mud, lime, and worms had reduced the remains to pieces of bone and rotted flesh. Although some corpses had been there for years, Russell Nelson's body had been in the crawl space just one year. From gruesome pictures, his mother was asked to identify her 21-year-old son, an honor student at the University of Minnesota who, at the time of his disappearance, had been preparing to get married. Gacy says he doesn't remember Russell.

Other identifications were possible mainly because of dental records and Gacy's collection of wallets and other belongings of his victims. Most of the young men were sexually assaulted and tortured before they were murdered.

In spite of his confession, Gacy soon declared his innocence. After his death sentence, he told his lawyers it was just "round one." In a telephone interview, he said, "There was no solid evidence that convicted me."

Gacy was one of more than 120 inmates waiting on death row in Illinois when, in September 1990, Charles Walker was executed—the first Illinois prisoner executed since 1962. Although Gacy has been on death row longer than most of

In 1980 John Wayne Gacy, Jr., right, *was convicted of killing 33 people. Police found the bodies of 29 victims buried in the crawl space of his house,* below.

Sam Amirante was one of John Wayne Gacy's defense lawyers. Gacy delayed the appeals process by repeatedly firing his lawyers.

the other inmates, he is not likely to be executed anytime soon. He claims to have health problems and is fairly certain he will die of natural causes.

"I'm afraid he might be right," Norma Nelson has said. The Nelsons are enraged by the lengthy appeals process in this case. Gacy has delayed the process by repeatedly firing his lawyers. Each time he fires a lawyer, more time is needed to start over with a new lawyer. Gacy has claimed his trial lawyers were incompetent due to their inexperience with mass-murder cases. He has also objected to their attempts to use an **insanity defense**. Most of Gacy's fees have been paid by federal and state programs for defendants who have little or no money.[2]

Since public opinion polls show strong support for capital punishment, John Wayne Gacy has often been used as an example by those who favor the death penalty and want to speed up the process. But is Gacy's case an extreme example, both in brutality and in the length of time involved in the appeals process? Perhaps. Still, his case clearly shows the potential for abusing the system. And it shows the costs—to the public, but especially to the victims' families.

For the Nelsons, losing a son was bad enough. But added to that is the devastating presence in their lives of someone like Gacy, a presence unlikely to be erased, even if he is executed. It seems sometimes that it is the Nelsons, and others in similar situations, who face the life sentence.

Mrs. Lola Woods, right, the mother of one of Gacy's victims, arrives for the start of the trial in Chicago, Illinois, 1980.

In 1938 a mob riddled W.C. Williams's body with bullets after hanging him from an oak tree in Rufton, Louisiana. He was captured by a mob of 300 people shortly after his arrest for assault and murder. The lynching took place just yards from the scene of the crime.

METHODS OF EXECUTION

In the past, justice in the United States has taken many different forms. Critics of the present, admittedly flawed, judicial system need only look back a few decades to see how much worse it used to be.

One day in 1959, several men changed for a few hours from respected, law-abiding residents of the town of Poplarville, Mississippi, into killers. They turned into a **lynch** mob. The term *lynching* refers to the illegal punishment of someone accused of a crime. Lynching involves an angry mob taking justice into its own hands.

A young black man in Poplarville named Mack Charles Parker had been arrested for the rape of a white woman. Shortly after Parker's arrest, the mob stormed the jail, beat him repeatedly, shot him, and threw his body into a nearby river. Most people in town knew who had participated in this crime, but no one was ever punished. This classic case of lynching was unusual only because it occurred so recently. It was one of the last lynchings in the United States.

For well over 100 years, white people in the United States lynched black people without worrying about being punished. The shocking stories are well documented—stories of

49

frenzied mobs setting black Americans on fire or hanging them from the nearest tree, stories of pregnant black women being hanged while their unborn babies were cut from their bodies and ripped apart, stories of accused rapists being mutilated.

Only after such spectacles drew the attention of shocked "outsiders" did it become good politics—politically advantageous—to oppose lynchings, and the phenomenon disappeared. However, many people feel that the administration of the death penalty is similar to lynchings, only more subtle, because death row houses a disproportionate number of blacks.

The history of lynchings can also be viewed as an argument in favor of capital punishment. Public opinion clearly shows the growing frustration with increasing violence in the United States. More and more people see the death penalty as a just reparation, or punishment, for violent crime. If executions were again discontinued, is it possible that an increase in lynchings and other forms of **vigilantism** would result?

JUSTICE ON DISPLAY

Lynchings were a public display of punishment in which citizens took "justice" into their own hands. Until the mid-1800s, virtually all legal executions were also held in public. Americans continued this long tradition in part to provide citizens with a chance to celebrate justice being done, much as the lynchings had done.

Public executions were also thought to serve as a warning to others against committing similar crimes, although this approach was anything but successful. During the executions, spectators often committed the same crimes for which the condemned person was being executed. Theft and assault were common occurrences during executions.[1]

Murder is only one of many crimes that have been punishable by death. In England, as recently as the early 1800s, there were about 200 capital offenses, including robbery, rape, and arson. And children were often executed, even those under 10. Although the American colonists did not punish as many crimes with death as did the English, the colonists borrowed many of the practices—such as hanging, beheading, burning alive, drowning, and stoning—that had been used in England for centuries.

Some methods of execution are nothing less than torture. Japanese criminals used to be killed with 21 cuts to the body, while in China people were boiled alive. The Spanish used the garrote, an iron collar tightened around the neck with a screw. English prisoners were pressed to death as late as 1777.[2]

"Drawing and quartering" was another practice, begun in England during the 14th century. This method called for the condemned person to be hanged (but not to death), disemboweled (often while conscious), beheaded, and then hacked into four quarters which could be put on display in some public place.[3]

A SEARCH FOR HUMANE METHODS OF EXECUTION
In the United States, in addition to demanding fewer capital offenses, reformers wanted the death penalty to be carried out in more humane ways than in the past. With this goal in mind, on August 6, 1890, New York State used a new method of execution—the electric chair. Even though it quickly became the most popular method of execution, some critics consider it to be only a modern version of burning someone

Public hanging, above, was a common form of execution until the mid-19th century. In England prisoners were "pressed" to death or until they confessed, right. The English also had an instrument similar to the French guillotine for beheading criminals, below.

at the stake. An observer of the first electrocution is reported to have said that he thought "the job could have been done better with an axe."[4]

Was this cruel and unusual punishment, as the lawyer of this first electrocuted prisoner unsuccessfully argued? The whole idea had been to make death as quick and painless as possible, but many people believe that no method of execution succeeds in this respect. Death by electrocution is not always quick, and the prisoner definitely feels pain. As recently as May 4, 1990, it took three separate 2,000-volt surges to kill a man, Jesse Tafero, in Florida. Fire, smoke, and sparks spewed from his head.[5]

Reports from numerous witnesses to electrocution appear to agree on many of the details. The electrodes attached to the shaved human head and leg reach temperatures higher than 1,900°F (1,093.3°C). This is hot enough to melt copper, so it's not surprising that it also brings the temperature of the human brain to the boiling point.[6]

When this much electricity shoots through human beings, their bodies involuntarily jerk and cringe, and eyeballs can literally pop out of the sockets.[7] It is common for prisoners to vomit blood and saliva as well as to lose control of their bodily functions. This ordeal is often prolonged and repeated. Sometimes the electrodes have to be refastened if the first surge of electricity burns through the flesh but does not kill the prisoner.[8] After death occurs, the contorted body has to be forcibly straightened in order to fit it into a coffin for burial.

Prior to the invention of the electric chair, the most common method of execution—in addition to hanging—was by firing squad. Traditionally a small group of skilled marksmen formed the squad. They aimed at a bullseye that was placed over the heart of the condemned prisoner. The prisoner was usually blindfolded. One of the rifles used by the firing squad was loaded with a blank to prevent individuals in the squad from feeling personal guilt for the killing. Smart riflemen, however, knew that the gun firing the blank would feel cooler than the others.[9]

Many people believe that shooting is one of the more humane methods of execution if the firing squad is skillful. But more "modern," less bloody methods seemed necessary by the turn of the century, if only to make the executioner's role more indirect. Only the state of Utah still uses a firing squad, and only if the condemned prisoner requests it, as did Gary Gilmore in 1977.

Another common method of execution is gassing. A gas chamber is a small, sealed room, in which the condemned person sits strapped to a metal chair. A lethal gas produced by combining several chemicals is released through a valve in the chamber floor. Normally it takes four to eight minutes for death to occur.

But things can go wrong. Jimmy Lee Gray, for example, died in the Mississippi gas chamber in 1983 after what witnesses described as a "desperate and fitful struggle for breath." They also stated that Gray "convulsed for eight minutes and his head kept striking a steel pole on the back of the chamber's walls."[10]

A few states, such as Texas, use **lethal injections.** But killing by injection presents its own complications. Amnesty International, an organization that is trying to end executions worldwide, keeps a list of botched executions that have taken place in the United States since 1979. Five of the eleven cases listed occurred in Texas through the use of injections.[11]

Method of execution, by state, 1989

Lethal injection

Arkansas[a, b]	Montana[a]	Oregon
Colorado	Nevada	South Dakota
Delaware	New Hampshire[a, d]	Texas
Idaho[a]	New Jersey	Utah[a]
Illinois	New Mexico	Washington[a]
Mississippi[a, c]	North Carolina[a]	Wyoming
Missouri[a]	Oklahoma	

Electrocution

Alabama	Indiana	Pennsylvania
Arkansas[a, b]	Kentucky	South Carolina
Connecticut	Louisiana	Tennessee
Florida	Nebraska	Virginia
Georgia	Ohio[e]	

Lethal gas

Arizona	Maryland	Missouri[a]
California	Mississippi[a, c]	North Carolina[a]

Hanging

Montana[a]	New Hampshire[a, d]	Washington[a]

Firing squad

Idaho[a]	Utah[a]

Note: Federal executions are to be carried out according to the method of the state in which they are performed.

[a] Authorizes 2 methods of execution

[b] Arkansas authorizes lethal injection for those whose capital offense occurred after 7/4/83; for those whose offense occurred before that date, the condemned prisoner may elect lethal injection or electrocution.

[c] Mississippi authorizes lethal injection for those convicted after 7/1/84; execution of those convicted prior to that date is to be carried out with lethal gas.

[d] New Hampshire authorizes hanging only if lethal injection could not be given.

[e] On 6/13/89 the Ohio legislature passed a bill to adopt lethal injection as the method of execution. This bill was vetoed by the governor on 7/3/89. Action to override the veto was pending in the legislature at year end.

Data Source: U.S. Department of Justice, Bureau of Justice Statistics

(A)

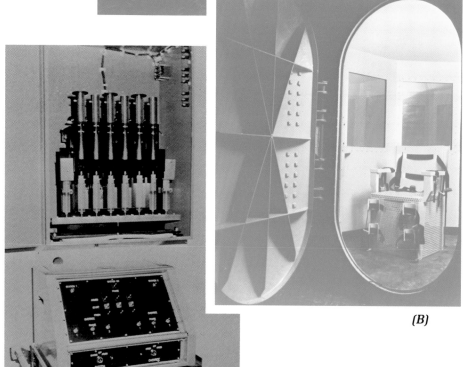

(B)

(C)

(D)

Current methods of execution in the United States include: the gas chamber, exterior (A) and interior (B); lethal injection (C); firing squad (D); and electric chair (E).

(E)

Prisoners under sentence of death, by region and state, year end 1988 and 1989

Region and state	Prisoners under sentence of death			Region and state	Prisoners under sentence of death		
	As of 1988	Executed in 1988	As of 1989		As of 1988	Executed in 1988	As of 1989
U.S. total[a]	2,117	16	2,250	South, cont'd.			
Federal	0	0	0	Georgia	91	1	90
State	2,117	16	2,250	Kentucky	32	0	29
				Louisiana	39	0	35
Northeast	124	0	132	Maryland	14	0	16
				Mississippi	47	1	44
Connecticut	1	0	2	North Carolina	79	0	88
New Hampshire	0	0	0	Oklahoma	99	0	109
New Jersey	21	0	18	South Carolina	35	0	42
Pennsylvania	102	0	112	Tennessee	70	0	75
				Texas	284	4	304
Midwest	337	1	345	Virginia	39	1	43
Illinois	115	0	115	West	410	2	463
Indiana	51	0	48				
Missouri	69	1	72	Arizona	78	0	84
Nebraska	13	0	12	California	228	0	254
Ohio	89	0	98	Colorado	3	0	3
South Dakota	0	0	0	Idaho	15	0	18
				Montana	7	0	8
South	1,246	13	1,310	Nevada	45	2	52
				New Mexico	2	0	1
Alabama	96	4	106	Oregon	15	0	23
Arkansas	27	0	33	Utah	8	0	11
Delaware	7	0	7	Washington	7	0	7
Florida	287	2	289	Wyoming	2	0	2

Note: States not listed and the District of Columbia did not authorize the death penalty as of 12/31/88.

[a]Excludes 5 males held under Armed Forces jurisdiction with a military death sentence for murder.

Data Source: U.S. Department of Justice, Bureau of Justice Statistics

Stephen Peter Morin died in 1985. It took technicians 45 minutes of sticking needles in both arms and legs to find a proper vein for the injection. Two minutes into the 1988 execution of Raymond Landry, the syringe popped out of his vein and sprayed blood and chemicals across the room. The injection was eventually resumed, but the procedure took 40 minutes. Other prisoners have had violent reactions to the drugs themselves and slowly choked to death.[12]

WEIGHING THE COSTS

If there is, in fact, no humane way to execute someone, should the ultimate punishment be life imprisonment without parole? Critics of this idea point to already over-populated prisons. They also object to the expense of a life sentence. They say that taxpayers do not want to support a killer for years and years. It would seem logical that shortening the life of a murderer would save millions of dollars. But, in fact, it is more expensive to execute. This cost is not because of the expense of the procedure itself. It is because of the lengthy appeals process (for which the public usually pays) and the special isolation and security required on death row. Some of the expense could be offset if death-row prisoners were at least allowed to work productively, but they are not.

A 1982 study by the New York State Defenders' Association calculated that the average capital trial and first stage of appeals cost the taxpayer about $1.8 million per case, about three times the cost of keeping a person in prison for life. In Kansas, the current cost of maintaining the death penalty is estimated to be $11 million a year. Because of appeals, one murderer, John Spenkelink, had cost the state of Florida somewhere between $5 million and $7 million by the time he was executed in 1979.[13]

President Richard Nixon (1969-1974), top, *President George Bush,* upper right, *Bill Clinton,* center right, *governor of Arkansas and a 1992 presidential contender, and Andrew Young,* below, *former congressman, mayor of Atlanta, Georgia, and ambassador to the United Nations, are just a few of the politicians who favor capital punishment.*

THE POLITICS
OF LIFE
AND DEATH

Although the debate over capital punishment is clouded by individual perceptions of right and wrong, of justice, and of revenge, one thing is becoming clear: a large segment of the U.S. public is clamoring for the death penalty. According to a 1966 Gallup poll, only about 42 percent of the population supported it, but by 1990 almost 80 percent supported the death penalty.[1] Why such an increase?

Part of the answer is the rise in violent crime. As Congressman James Traficant of Ohio expressed it in his support of stricter crime laws: "The U.S. does not lead the world in education, trade, and health care, but we lead in murder. We are the killing fields of the world."[2]

But another reason for supporting capital punishment involves a lack of public trust in "the system." Many people think current laws are too lenient and often ignored. Enforcement is sometimes delayed beyond reasonable limits, and long procedural delays cause the death-row population to grow at an alarming rate. The public seems to be losing trust not only in the courts' ability to put and keep prisoners behind bars but also in the ability of the police to catch criminals in the first place.[3]

Presidents, crime and punishment

Administration	Imprisonment	Felony crimes (annual average)	Probability of imprisonment (percentage)
Eisenhower 1953-1961	2,567,398	81,643	3.18%
Kennedy 1961-1963	3,783,223	90,140	2.38
Johnson 1963-1969	5,430,226	80,570	1.48
Nixon 1969-1974	8,211,400	99,784	1.22
Ford 1974-1977	10,938,290	120,936	1.11
Carter 1977-1981	11,879,100	131,835	1.11
Reagan 1981-1989	12,677,135	184,828	1.46

Data Source: National Center for Policy Analysis

THE VOTERS DECIDE

The United States has had a long history of political tur-
moil over such issues. Over the past two decades, liberal
Democrats have been viewed as being "soft" on crime.
During his 1968 presidential campaign, Republican Richard
Nixon cried out for "law and order." Voters listened to
conservative Republican promises and voted their agree-
ment. Republicans won five of the seven presidential
elections between 1964 and 1988, although the crime rate
has continued to rise.[4]

Partly because of the "law and order" mood of the country,
it has become good politics to support the death penalty.
Candidates for public office appeal to voters by voicing their
impatience with the way things are and offering tough, new
solutions. Even committed liberals like Atlanta's former
mayor Andrew Young, a nonviolent disciple of Martin Luther
King, Jr., have changed their minds on the issue in favor of

harsher, swifter justice. "This seems to be the only thing that people have any faith in," explained Young as a candidate for governor of Georgia. "The state has got to have the right to put mad dogs to death."[5]

Expressing a similar sentiment, Dianne Feinstein, while running for governor of California, said, "We have reached the point where some, by their acts, do give up the right to survive."

One of the biggest political changes to develop in regard to the death penalty is the position many African-Americans have taken. Although they used to oppose capital punishment by almost three to one, the majority now supports it. "In 1990, crime is no longer polarizing," says Geoffrey Garin, a political expert. "The demand for tough law enforcement unites blacks and whites, liberals and conservatives, across the board."[7]

Some liberal politicians, however, have not changed their views about the death penalty. They criticize candidates who indulge the public's worst instincts, just to get elected. Vic Kamber, a Democratic consultant, complains: "Both parties have opted for the easy way out—give voters what they want in terms of instant gratification, including instant death." He adds that, although it can be emotionally satisfying to some, the death penalty can never solve the violent-crime problem in this country.[8] On the other hand, the increasing support for capital punishment does reflect public opinion and shifting social attitudes.

WIDENING THE "DEATH BELT"

Most executions still occur in southern states, sometimes referred to as the "death belt." However, California has become a focal point of the death-penalty debate because of the case of Robert Alton Harris. Harris appears to be an ideal candidate for execution, and his case is often used to argue for the death penalty. His crime took place in San Diego on July 5, 1978, just six months after he had completed a two-and-a-half-year prison term for beating a man to death. His victims this time were two teenage boys.

Harris and his brother Danny decided to steal the boys' car, which they spotted at a fast-food restaurant. Harris kidnapped the teenagers, then shot and killed them. Later he calmly ate their unfinished hamburgers. Danny testified against his brother and served three years in federal prison.[9]

If Harris goes to the gas chamber, California—traditionally a fairly liberal state—will join the short list of states that have carried out executions since the Supreme Court declared the death penalty constitutional in 1976. Harris's execution may occur during a period when the death penalty is a hot campaign issue around the country. According to the chairman of the National Coalition to Abolish the Death Penalty, "There is almost a mob attitude in California, a frenzy being fed by politicians."[10]

If California joins Illinois in resuming executions, experts wonder whether other states with capital-punishment statutes, such as Ohio and Pennsylvania, could be far behind. The momentum could build until a majority of states have responded to the demands of their residents.*

---

*Robert Alton Harris was executed in California's gas chamber at 6:05 A.M. on Tuesday, April 21, 1992.

Number of persons executed by state in rank order, 1930-1989

State	Number executed		State	Number executed	
	1930-1989	1977-1989		1930-1989	1977-1989
Georgia	380	14	Federal System	33	—
Texas	330	33	Nevada	33	4
New York	329	—	Massachusetts	27	—
California	292	—	Connecticut	21	—
North Carolina	266	3	Oregon	19	—
Florida	191	21	Iowa	18	—
Ohio	172	—	Utah	16	3
South Carolina	164	2	Kansas	15	—
Mississippi	158	4	Delaware	12	—
Pennsylvania	152	—	New Mexico	8	—
Louisiana	151	18	Wyoming	7	—
Alabama	142	7	Montana	6	—
Arkansas	118	—	Vermont	4	—
Kentucky	103	—	Nebraska	4	—
Virginia	100	8	Idaho	3	—
Tennessee	93	—	South Dakota	1	—
Illinois	90	—	New Hampshire	1	—
New Jersey	74	—	Wisconsin	0	—
Maryland	68	—	Rhode Island	0	—
Missouri	63	1	North Dakota	0	—
Oklahoma	60	—	Minnesota	0	—
Washington	47	—	Michigan	0	—
Colorado	47	—	Maine	0	—
Indiana	43	2	Hawaii	0	—
West Virginia	40	—	Alaska	0	—
District of Columbia	40	—			
			U.S. total	3,979	120
Arizona	38	—			

Data Source: U.S. Department of Justice, Bureau of Justice Statistics

John Spenkelink, above, and James Dupree Henry, left, were executed for murder. Did their deaths deter others from killing? Paul LaVergne, Thomas Varnum, and Robert Douglas Hill, below, left to right, are on death row. If they are killed, will other potential murderers be deterred?

DEATH AND DETERRENCE

Most people would probably agree that it's better to focus on preventing crimes before they happen than it is to focus on punishing the criminal after the crime has been committed. But how do we prevent, or deter, murder? Does the prospect of having to face execution for a murder keep at least some people from killing?

If **deterrence** could be proven to everyone's satisfaction, arguments in favor of capital punishment would be greatly strengthened. After all, preventing innocent people from becoming victims certainly seems to justify executing the guilty. But the evidence appears to fall evenly on both sides of this argument.

One of the most important studies about the deterrent effect of capital punishment was conducted by researcher and New York University professor Isaac Ehrlich. His results were published in the *American Economic Review* in 1975. Ehrlich concluded, based on statistics gathered between 1933 and 1969, that each execution prevents about seven or eight people from committing murder.[1]

In 1985 Stephen K. Layson, an economist at the University of North Carolina published a study that appeared to prove

67

that every execution of a murderer deters, on the average, 18 murderers who would otherwise have killed their victims. The study further suggests that raising even the number of murder **convictions** by 1 percent would prevent 105 murders. Currently only 38 percent of all murder cases result in a conviction. And of those convicted murderers, only 0.1 percent are executed.[2]

Critics of these and other studies point out, however, that so many factors enter into individual acts of murder that statistical studies cannot possibly take everything into account. What about the homicides that result from emotional outbursts, for example? Does it make sense that a person in a murderous rage would necessarily stop to think about what his or her chances are of being executed?

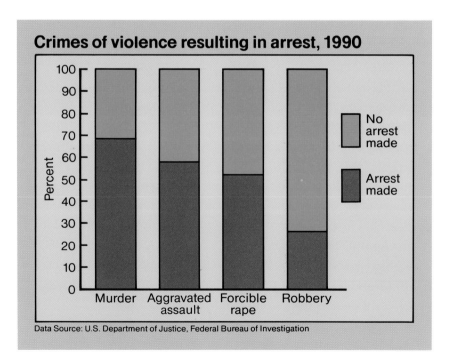

Crimes of violence resulting in arrest, 1990

Data Source: U.S. Department of Justice, Federal Bureau of Investigation

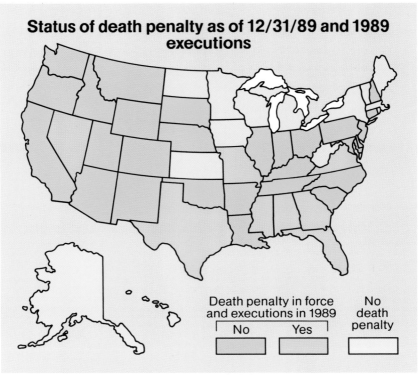

Status of death penalty as of 12/31/89 and 1989 executions

Death penalty in force and executions in 1989: No / Yes

No death penalty

Data Source: U.S. Department of Justice, Bureau of Justice Statistics

Setting murder rate statistics aside, the question must be asked, What deters a person who *might*—but *doesn't*—commit murder? The death penalty—"if you do this, you might die for it"—may simply add to a person's built-in resistance to doing such a thing.

Steven Goldberg, a sociology professor at City College in New York, summed it up in an article for the *National Review*: "Potential murderers simply act; the deterrent effect of the death penalty, if there is one, acts upon them. If it acts with sufficient strength, it prevents their becoming murderers."[3] In other words, a person in a position to murder may not *consciously* think of the death penalty, but it can be one of many factors that contribute to the prevention of the crime. Death is final, so it seems obvious that people—even potential murderers—fear death more than life imprisonment. The best deterrent is probably whatever is most feared.

Death-penalty advocates say that the evidence clearly shows that capital punishment deters murders more than other punishments do. With other kinds of illegal acts, such as traffic violations, increasing the penalties does appear to decrease the number of violations.

On the other hand, critics of the death penalty can point to as many studies that show no link at all between executions and the prevention of future murders. In fact,

Melvin Powell is a death-row inmate in California's San Quentin Prison. Is a lifetime behind bars better than death by execution?

some experts believe that capital punishment has a "brutalizing effect" that *increases* the level of violence in society. Murder rates may actually go up instead of down because of the death penalty.[4]

It is also possible that, for some people, the prospect of being killed because of something they do may really heighten their excitement about doing it. The possibility of death adds to the challenge of racing cars and climbing mountains. Some murderers might feel the same way about killing.[5]

Whether opinions are formed on the basis of common sense or decades of formal studies, the relationship between capital punishment and deterrence is still not clear. Maybe this is because there are so few executions compared to the number of murders. And because there are so few executions, it might be impossible to measure their deterrent effect.

Some death-penalty advocates say, however, that regardless of what statistics show, if there's *any* chance of preventing future homicides by executing convicted murderers, why not do it? Aren't the lives of even a few potential victims more precious than those of murderers?[6]

Some people argue that looking at the deterrent effect of any one method of punishment is useless when so many crimes in this country—an estimated 97.5 percent—result in no punishment at all.[7] How can the crime rate go anywhere but up under these conditions? If crime continues to go unpunished, what will keep individuals from doing whatever they want, even killing?

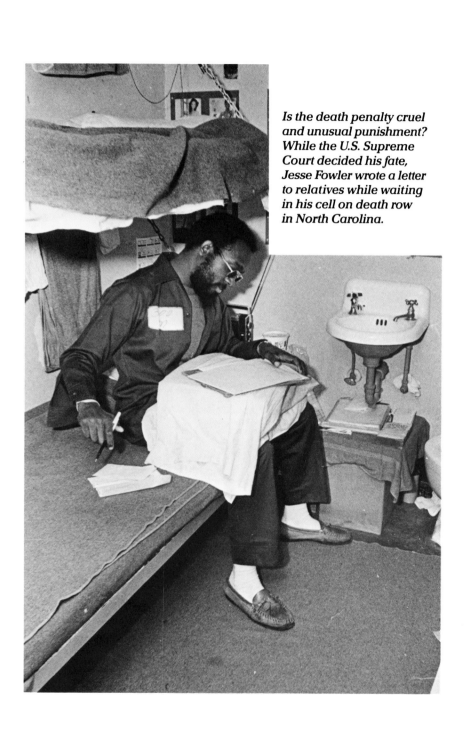

Is the death penalty cruel and unusual punishment? While the U.S. Supreme Court decided his fate, Jesse Fowler wrote a letter to relatives while waiting in his cell on death row in North Carolina.

CRUEL AND UNUSUAL?

Arguments against capital punishment most often have to do with morality—right and wrong—and with fairness. Many of those who would like to abolish capital punishment argue that it is simply *wrong* for the state to kill, regardless of what crimes a person has committed. And they argue that in the United States, the death sentence has been given disproportionately to nonwhite, usually poor people.

From a moral viewpoint, capital punishment raises many questions about the sanctity of human life—the belief that human life has great value, regardless of what crimes a person might commit. This idea is fundamental to many religions. For Christians and Jews, it has its origin in the Bible, especially in the Old Testament, which says that "God created man in his own image."

HUMAN RIGHTS

Since, in most countries, human life is believed to have an inherent value, many governing bodies have established laws based on a belief in human rights. The most important right of all has been established as the right to live.[1] When the death penalty is being debated, these beliefs that human life is sacred and that everyone has an equal right to life can be used to support both sides of the debate. Many of those opposed to the death penalty argue that nobody's life should be deliberately taken by the state or anyone else. Those who support the death penalty argue that capital punishment, the most severe sentence possible, is justified when someone has taken a human life.

Do murderers, by their acts, forfeit their right to life? Many people believe they do. Certain rights are often taken away for the good of society. For example, isn't a person's fundamental right to freedom taken away if she or he robs a bank and is imprisoned?

But does anyone deserve to die? If the goal is to match the punishment to the crime—to give everyone the punishment they deserve—then how do we deal with sadistic individuals who torture before killing, or those who kill dozens of people?

Dr. George N. Boyd, a professor of religion, says that "the capital-punishment debate is not about what murderers deserve, but rather about how society should express and defend its fundamental values. . . ." For Dr. Boyd, the best argument against the death penalty is "that society best expresses its cherishing of life by abstaining from taking even the life that deserves to be taken. . . ." This argument springs, in part, from the traditional Christian belief that God is so loving and merciful that no one is actually punished as severely as he or she deserves.[2]

But is it impossible for murderers ever to make adequate reparation, to pay for their crimes? Dr. Boyd feels it is dangerous to give criminals the comforting illusion that reparation *is* possible. He also says that the only way to prevent the execution of the innocent—as immoral an act as any done by a murderer—is to execute no one.[3]

The possibility of racism in the judicial system also raises a question of morality. Warren McCleskey was a black man arrested in 1978 and condemned to death for the murder of a white police officer. As part of his appeal, a team of lawyers and statisticians showed that killers of whites were four times as likely to be given a death sentence in Georgia than killers of blacks. In *McCleskey v. the State of Georgia,* probably the most important death-penalty case of the 1980s, this apparent inequality was brought before the U.S. Supreme Court.

In April 1987, after bitter debate, the Court split its vote five to four, rejecting the legal challenge to Georgia's death-penalty practices. Five justices acknowledged a "discrepancy that appears to correlate with race," but they ruled that there was no clear evidence of racial bias in McCleskey's trial. Justice Lewis F. Powell, Jr., wrote for the majority: "Apparent disparities in sentencing are an inevitable part of our criminal justice system."[4]

The opinions of the four justices who disagreed—William J. Brennan, Jr., Thurgood Marshall, Harry A. Blackmun and John Paul Stevens—are significant because of their insistence that the evidence was indeed great that racism has stained the capital-punishment system. Justice Brennan concluded his unusually strong statement by saying that the process "reflects a devaluation of the lives of black persons."[5] McCleskey was executed on September 25, 1991.

In a more recent decision—to halt the execution of a convicted murderer in Virginia—Justice Brennan wrote that taking a human life "is God's work, not man's. . . . The most vile murder does not, in my view, release the state from constitutional restraints on the destruction of human dignity."[6]

William Rehnquist, Chief Justice of the U.S. Supreme Court, wants limits put on the appeals process in cases involving the death penalty.

IN THE COURTROOM

Judges, lawyers, and juries are a necessary part of our judicial system. Sometimes they also carry the heavy responsibility of deciding who should live and who should die.

Judges have an enormous impact on the lives of criminals and their victims. A judge can affect the tone, or disposition, of a trial. He or she gives instructions to the jurors and rules on the objections from attorneys during the course of a trial. In some states, a jury is asked to recommend a sentence, but the judge makes the final decision.

Florida is one state that allows a judge to override a jury's recommendation for life imprisonment rather than death. Since the 10-year moratorium ended, the death penalty has been imposed in Florida in about 20 percent of the cases in which the jury had recommended life imprisonment. The judges in those cases imposed the death penalty.[1]

Of course judges are human and have opinions like the rest of the population. Some judges favor and some oppose the death penalty. They have duties to carry out, however, and sometimes they have to carry them out in spite of their beliefs. If the law requires it in his or her state, a judge who is opposed to capital punishment may be forced to sentence a convicted criminal to death. Likewise, a judge who favors capital punishment may have to be satisfied with life imprisonment as the most severe sentence possible.

ON THE JURY

Judges have studied and worked long and hard to take on such life-and-death responsibilities. Most judges probably believe strongly in the judicial system and want to serve it to the best of their abilities. But what about juries? They are made up of people who have varying abilities, probably little knowledge of the law, and little choice about serving as a juror.

What is it like to be a member of a jury in a murder case? Even if you are only 1 of 12, how does it feel to hold a person's fate in your hands? Looking at one particular jury in one case may provide some answers.

In the 1983 trial of David Steffen, jurors were faced with a good-looking, soft-spoken young man charged with a vicious murder. Prosecutors alleged that while selling cleaning products door-to-door, Steffen entered the Cincinnati home of 19-year-old Karen Range. While inside, he raped her and cut her throat with a knife from her kitchen.

Testimony at the trial showed that Steffen had a history of arrests and imprisonment both as a juvenile and as an adult. His childhood had been filled with beatings and other cruel and humiliating treatment from his stepfather.

After a trial that lasted two weeks, the jury of 10 women and 2 men found Steffen guilty and recommended the death penalty. The judge agreed and sentenced him to the electric chair.

All the jurors selected for Steffen's trial were "death qualified." In other words, they had stated a belief in capital punishment. (Using only death-qualified jurors, as demanded by prosecuting attorneys, is common at murder trials, but it is a controversial practice that is being called into question.)[2]

Even with an established belief in the death penalty, however, one juror spoke for several of them when she told a reporter after the trial that serving on this case was "traumatic. It was terrible, and I'm still shaken. I just hope I never have to go through something like that again." Asked about the death penalty, she cried and said, "I didn't want to do it, but I had to."

About six months after the trial, many of the jurors continued to show stress from their experience. Symptoms included disturbed sleep, memory impairment, and depression.

The jurors got to know the intimate details of Steffen's life, details that inspired as much pity as anger. As one juror stated, "I don't feel I have the authority to say when a man should die. . . . I know Mr. Steffen personally [from the trial]. He almost becomes a friend. . . . But he murdered this girl and society expects restitution."

Several jurors used the word "killing" to describe what they ended up having to do to Steffen. The following comments from one tearful juror are typical: "I was doing the right thing, but it was a horrible thing to do. It would be on my conscience if he hurt someone else. . . . Well, when you heard the horrible things about his childhood. . . . That's when you feel sorry for him. . . feel that if somebody gave him some love at an early age. Now, it's hopeless."

The biggest factor in the jurors' decision for the death penalty was their feelings about Steffen's potential future behavior. They felt he would pose a danger to the public if he were ever allowed to go free, which he probably would with a sentence of life imprisonment. Although convinced

During the Sylvia Seegrist murder trial, an armed police matron escorted the jury to lunch across the street from the courthouse.

A defense attorney shows a photograph to the jury during a rape trial. The presiding judge, Mary Lupo, and the court reporter are seated to the right.

they had done the right thing, most of the jurors still felt guilty about their decision.[3]

THE LAWYERS

Other major participants in any courtroom are the attorneys, at least one for the prosecution and one for the defense. Prosecuting attorneys are expected to prove that the accused is guilty, even if they are unconvinced of the defendant's guilt. Defense attorneys are expected to defend the innocence of their clients, even if they know that person is guilty.

As already noted, most death-row inmates have court-appointed attorneys. According to a 1990 investigation conducted by the National Law Journal, the lawyers who represent capital-punishment cases are likely to be either the most inexperienced, the most disillusioned and indifferent, or the most unethical.

Of course, not all death-row inmates have inept defense lawyers. Many attorneys work tirelessly on behalf of their clients. When the death penalty is involved, some attorneys dedicate themselves to a case because they feel strongly that no prisoner should be killed. David Bruck is such an attorney. On a typical day, he has to travel through tunnels, security checks, and steel doors in order to do what he does regularly—visit death row.

"Da-VID!" one of the prisoners calls out from his tiny cell. Bruck smiles and stops to chat, to grasp the hands that reach out between the bars. He devotes most of his time to defending prisoners who face death sentences. Along with a handful of other lawyers defending inmates on death row, Bruck works mainly in the "death belt" of the Deep South.

On this day, David Bruck has come to talk to Dale Robert Yates, who is brought to him in chains by guards. Two days earlier, Bruck had argued Yates's case before the U.S. Supreme Court in an attempt to win a new trial. They exchange warm, although weary, greetings. In 1981 Yates and another man held up a store in South Carolina. A woman was stabbed to death by the other man, but Yates was also convicted of murder and sentenced to death.

Lawyers opposed to the death penalty admit that, in many of their cases, they have no doubt that their death-row clients are guilty. But they believe that killing *anybody* is wrong, despite the Supreme Court ruling, despite how the public feels.

Since death-row inmates usually have no money for legal fees, the state assigns lawyers who typically get a fee of only $1,000 per case. The most David Bruck gets from the state of South Carolina is $2,500 for a death-row case. A 1987 survey for the American Bar Association showed that in 114 death-penalty cases in 24 states, defense lawyers worked an average of 2,000 hours without pay over a two-year period.

Their job is to win time for their clients, and that can best be done by creating doubt about a case, searching for small points of law that can cast a different light on the facts and make it possible for a court or a governor to grant mercy. They play up evidence of brain disorders or permanent effects of childhood abuse. Perhaps circumstances surrounding the crime itself, or the arrest, can be further explored.

Defense attorneys are frequently asked, "How can you defend people like that?" Many answer by saying that everyone is entitled to a defense, even those who can't afford one and those who have committed the most horrible crimes. Sometimes they add that they have not found most condemned persons to be that much different from you and me.[4]

"SOMEBODY HAS TO DO IT"

> *"I'm just carrying out a job, doing what I was asked to do. . . . This man has been sentenced to death in the courts. This is the law and he broke this law, and he has to suffer the consequences."*
> *—a member of an execution team*[1]

It's one thing to believe in capital punishment, but how, you might wonder, can anybody actually perform the job of executing people? Who would do such work?

A common image of executioners is that of grim, frightening men in black hoods. With the introduction of the electric chair in 1890, however, it became necessary to hire executioners with not only a willingness to kill for hire but also knowledge of electricity.

The first official electrocutioner was a professional electrician named Edwin F. Davis. He helped design the electric chair and spent much of his 24 years as executioner improving the apparatus. Davis wore a distinctive, black hat and coat. He often used a chunk of beef to test the electrodes, which he carried throughout the eastern states. Over the years, Davis earned $10,000 for executing more than 240 persons.[2]

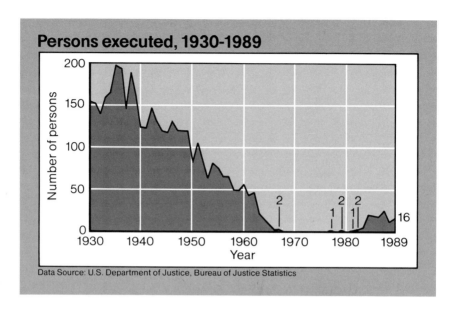

Persons executed, 1930-1989

Data Source: U.S. Department of Justice, Bureau of Justice Statistics

The peak period for executions in the United States occurred during the 1920s and 1930s. Executioner Robert G. Elliott, who had been trained by Davis, became well known by the public. A thin man with white hair and a deeply lined face, Elliott often executed several persons in a single day. In his 13 years as official executioner, Elliott earned $57,000 and electrocuted 387 people, 5 of them women.[3] Ironically, both Davis and Elliott were opposed to capital punishment.

But now most executioners work in teams, so that the job is carefully divided and no one person is totally responsible for the killing. The team spends a considerable amount of time with the condemned, in many states at least 24 hours before the execution. They work to fulfill the final needs of the condemned, along with the demands of the state.

For their own psychological well-being, however, members of the team avoid getting to know the condemned prisoners; they try to be polite but distant. The attitude of most executioners is "that the prisoners arrive as strangers and are easier to kill if they stay that way."[4]

The team's duties are clear. Last phone calls have to be made, last meals served, personal belongings inventoried and boxed. Prisoners must be kept calm and prevented from committing suicide. They must undergo some physical preparation for execution, such as the shaving necessary for electrocution. The procedure itself must be carried out with machinelike precision.

One officer on the execution team said, "We all take part in it; we all play 100 percent in it too. That takes the load off this one individual [who pulls the switch]."[5]

The final duty of the death team is preparing the prisoner's body for the morgue.

Some execution-team members experience stress related to their job; others do not. They go about their lives, ordinary people who are trained to do a job as skillfully and humanely as possible. One even said to a witness to an execution, "When I go home after one of these things, I sleep like a rock."[6]

Executioners work as part of a team ready to carry out their job.

EPILOGUE

Death is not a pleasant topic, especially deliberate, violent death. A murder and a legal execution can both be seen as deliberate and violent killing, depending on your point of view.

In the most simple terms, the debate over capital punishment involves the basic human right to *live*. Does everyone deserve this right, or should some, by taking that right away from others, be forced to give it up themselves?

Death is final. Some innocent people are, undoubtedly, executed, and some guilty ones are set free to kill again. These are hard facts to deal with, and they are among the facts that make the death penalty a difficult choice. But some see it as the best choice.

In the last decade of the 20th century, executions in the United States appear to be on the rise. This trend is occurring because the American public demands it. Most people sentenced to death are young, male, and poor. A disproportionate number are black. Is this a reflection of who commits the most murders, or is it due to unfairness in the judicial system?

Should the long, slow, costly appeals process be shortened and simplified? Or should a convicted murderer retain every opportunity to appeal that currently exists? As a taxpayer, now or in the future, are you willing to pay for the lengthy appeals process? Are you willing to risk an innocent person's life in order to streamline the system? What if someone you knew were arrested for murder? Would that change your opinion about capital punishment? As future judges, lawyers, jurors, and voting citizens, your opinion is important.

Meanwhile, even as you read this, acts of violence are being committed. The shock and sadness these acts cause will spread well beyond the times and places of the crimes. The victims' friends and relatives will begin their "life sentences," and, if caught, the murderers may be imprisoned to begin theirs. Others will spend years on death row contemplating their actions and the consequences of those actions, including death.

Endnotes

CHAPTER 1. ONE LIFE FOR ANOTHER

[1] George Hackett et al., "Indiana Killer, Italian Martyr," *Newsweek*, September 21, 1987, 37.

[2] Steven V. Roberts et al., "A Growing Cry: 'Give Them Death'," *U.S. News and World Report*, March 26, 1990, 24.

[3] Ned Zeman, "Pessimism," *Newsweek*, December 24, 1990, 6.

[4] Hackett, 37.

[5] Ibid.

[6] Fred Bruning, "Countdown to the Electric Chair," *Macleans*, October 26, 1987, 13.

[7] Ibid.

[8] Robert H. Loeb, Jr., *Crime and Capital Punishment* (New York: Franklin Watts, 1978), 28.

[9] Michael L. Radelet, *Facing the Death Penalty* (Philadelphia: Temple University Press, 1989), 3.

[10] Loeb, 6.

[11] Radelet, 3.

[12] Editorial, *Star Tribune* (Minneapolis), July 26, 1990, 22A.

[13] Roberts, 24.

[14] Kathryn Kahler, "Murderer at 15, Saved from Execution . . . ," *St. Paul Pioneer Press*, September 16, 1990, 4G.

CHAPTER 2. A LIVING DEATH

[1] Robert Johnson, *Condemned to Die* (New York: Elsevier Science Publisher, 1981), 41.

[2] Ibid., 44.

[3] Ibid., 17.

[4] Joseph M. Giarratano, "The Pains of Life," *Facing the Death Penalty* (1989), 195.

[5] Aaron Epstein, "Death Penalty Reversal Blame Put on Lawyers," *St. Paul Pioneer Press* (June 9, 1991), 10A.

[6] Aric Press et al., "Gridlock on Death Row," *Newsweek*, May 4, 1987, 61.

[7] Johnson, 18.

[8] David Kaplan et al., "Breaking the Death Barrier," *Newsweek*, February 19, 1990, 73.

[9] Mark A. Siegel et al., eds., *Capital Punishment: Cruel and Unusual?* (Wylie, Texas: Information Aids, Inc., 1988), 48.

[10] Lawrence A. Greenfeld, *Capital Punishment 1989.* (Washington, D.C.: Bureau of Justice Statistics, 1989), 7.

[11] Johnson, 1.

[12] Ginny Carroll et al., "Only Two Weeks to Live," *Newsweek*, August 21, 1989, 62-64.

CHAPTER 3. NO EXCEPTIONS?

[1] Aric Press et al., "Execution at an Early Age," *Newsweek*, January 13, 1986, 74.

[2] Alain L. Sanders, "Bad News for Death Row," *Time*, July 10, 1989, 48.

[3] Fred Bruning, "Countdown to the Electric Chair," *Macleans*, October 26, 1987, 13.

[4] Press, 74.

[5] Kathryn Kahler, "Juvenile Murderers Face Death," *St. Paul Pioneer Press*, September 16, 1990, 1G.

[6] "Abuse, Alcohol and Drugs Turn More Kids into Killers, Expert Says," *Star Tribune* (Minneapolis), August 14, 1990, 7A.

[7] Ibid., 7A.

[8] Ibid., 7A.

[9] Kahler, 5G.

[10] Sanders, 48.

[11] David Margolick, "Chair Closes in on Death Row 'Lawyer,'" *Star Tribune* (Minneapolis), March 6, 1990, 2A.

[12] "Rehnquist Backs Stricter Limit on Death Row Appeals," *Star Tribune* (Minneapolis), May 16, 1990, 15A.

[13] Ibid., 15A.

CHAPTER 4. JUSTICE OR REVENGE?

[1] Edward I. Koch, "Death and Justice," *New Republic*, April 15, 1985, 13-15.

[2] "Murder USA," *48 Hours*, September 13, 1990.

[3] Koch, 14.

[4] Ibid., 14.

[5] Ibid., 15.

[6] Ernest Van Den Haag, "Death and Deterrence," *National Review*, March 14, 1986, 44.

[7] "Death-Row Murderers Could Be Lifesavers," *Newsweek*, January 9, 1989, 49.

CHAPTER 5. FAMILIES OF VICTIMS—A "LIFE SENTENCE"

[1] Pat Doyle, "Trial Goes on for Family of Slain Student as Gacy Still Sits on Death Row," *Star Tribune* (Minneapolis), March 26, 1990, 1A and 6A.

[2] Ibid.

CHAPTER 6. METHODS OF EXECUTION

[1] Robert H. Loeb, Jr., *Crime and Capital Punishment* (New York: Franklin Watts, 1978), 14.

[2] Robert Pittman, "Electric Chair Marks a Century of Use—and It Still Seems Cruel and Unusual," *Star Tribune* (Minneapolis), August 15, 1990, 19A.

[3] Loeb, 18.

[4] Russell F. Canan, "Burning at the Wire," *Facing the Death Penalty*, ed. Michael L. Radelet (Philadelphia: Temple University Press, 1989), 67.

[5] Peter H. Gunst et al., "Even Murderers Don't Deserve Death by Torture," *Star Tribune* (Minneapolis), August 15, 1990.

[6] Canan, 67-68.

[7] Ibid.

[8] Ibid.

[9] Frederick Drimmer, *Until You Are Dead: The Book of Executions in America* (New York: Citadel Press, 1990), 91.

[10] Gunst, 19A.

[11] Pittman, 19A.

[12] Ibid.

[13] Richard C. Dieter, "The Death Penalty Dinosaur," *Commonweal*, January 15, 1988, 13.

CHAPTER 7. THE POLITICS OF LIFE AND DEATH

[1] Steven V. Roberts et al., "A Growing Cry: 'Give Them Death,'" *U.S. News and World Report* (March 26, 1990), 25.

[2] Ibid., 24.

[3] Ibid., 25.

[4] Ibid.

[5] Ibid.

[6] Ibid.

[7] Ibid.

[8] Ibid.

[9] Richard Lacayo, "The Politics of Life and Death," *Time*, April 2, 1990, 18.

[10] Ibid., 19.

CHAPTER 8. DEATH AND DETERRENCE

[1] Steven Goldberg, "So What if the Death Penalty Deters?" *National Review*, June 30, 1989, 42.

[2] Ernest Van Den Haag, "Death and Deterrence," *National Review*, March 14, 1986, 44.

[3] Goldberg, 42.

[4] Howard Zehr, "Capital Punishment Does Not Deter," *Reviving the Death Penalty*, eds. Gary E. McCuen and R.A. Baumgart (Hudson, Wisconsin: Gary McCuen Publications, Inc., 1985), 58.

[5] George N. Boyd, "Capital Punishment: Deserved and Wrong," *The Christian Century*, February 17, 1988, 163.

[6] Van Den Haag, 44.

[7] Walter Berns, "A Conservative Case in Favor of the Death Penalty," *Reviving the Death Penalty*, 90.

CHAPTER 9. CRUEL AND UNUSUAL?

[1] Hugo Adam Bedau, *Death Is Different* (Boston: Northeastern University Press, 1987), 10.

[2] George N. Boyd, "Capital Punishment: Deserved and Wrong," *The Christian Century*, February 17, 1988, 163-164.

[3] Boyd, 164.

[4] Aric Press et al., "Gridlock on Death Row," *Newsweek* (May 4, 1987), 60.

[5] Ibid.

[6] Peter H. Gunst et al., "Even Murderers Don't Deserve Death by Torture," *Star Tribune* (Minneapolis), August 15, 1990, 19A.

CHAPTER 10. IN THE COURTROOM

[1] Michael L. Radelet, ed., *Facing the Death Penalty* (Philadelphia: Temple University Press, 1989), 5.

[2] Phoebe Ellsworth, "Juries on Trial," *Psychology Today*, July, 1985, 44-46.

[3] Stanley M. Kaplan, "Death, So Say We All," *Psychology Today*, July, 1985, 48-53.

[4] David G. Stout, "The Lawyers of Death Row," *New York Times Magazine*, February 14, 1988, 46-54.

CHAPTER 11. "SOMEBODY HAS TO DO IT"

[1] Robert Johnson, "This Man Has Expired," *Commonweal*, January, 1989, 11.

[2] Frederick Drimmer, *Until You Are Dead: The Book of Executions in America* (New York: Citadel Press, 1990), 28-29.

[3] Ibid., 33.

[4] Ibid., 12.

[5] Ibid., 10.

[6] Ibid., 15.

Glossary

advocate: a person who speaks or writes in support of someone or of some cause, especially in court

appeal: to call upon a higher court of law to review the decision of a lower one

brief: a concise statement or outline of a client's case in a trial

capital offense: a crime legally punishable by the death penalty

conviction: the act of convicting someone of a crime in a court of law

death row: the section of a prison set aside to house inmates sentenced to death

desensitized: a state of decreased sensitivity to something because of frequent exposure to it

deterrence: discouraging or preventing an act because of the consequences of that act

felony: a serious crime, carrying stiffer penalties than a misdemeanor

homicide: the killing of one human being by another, whether murder or manslaughter

insanity defense: the argument that a defendant did not have the mental capability to determine the difference between right and wrong and therefore should not be held responsible for a crime committed

lethal injection: the injection of substances into a person's blood stream to cause death

lynch: to take the law into one's own hands and kill someone as punishment for a real or presumed crime

manslaughter: the unlawful killing of a human being without planning it ahead of time and without malicious intent

moratorium: an authorized halt of or delay of something

parole: the conditional release of a prisoner

rehabilitation: the restoration of physical and/or mental health through training; for criminals, the ability to live outside of institutions in accordance with the law

restitution: giving something as an equivalent for what has been damaged or taken

serial killer: a person who murders a number of victims, one after another–in a series

stay of execution: an order to stop or delay an execution

supremacy: superiority, right to dominate

unconstitutional: not in accordance with or supported by the U.S. Constitution

vigilantism: the suppression and punishment of crimes by a self-appointed group that acts when the process of law seems inadequate

Bibliography

Books

Amnesty International. *When the State Kills . . . The Death Penalty: A Human Rights Issue.* New York: Amnesty International USA, 1989.

Bedau, Hugo Adam. *Death is Different, Studies in the Morality, Law, and Politics of Capital Punishment.* Boston: Northeastern University Press, 1987.

Drimmer, Frederick. *Until You Are Dead: The Book of Executions in America.* New York: Citadel Press, Carol Publishing Group, 1990.

Johnson, Robert. *Condemned to Die, Life Under Sentence of Death.* New York: Elsevier Science Publisher, 1981.

Lester, David. *The Death Penalty, Issues and Answers.* Springfield, Illinois: Charles C. Thomas, 1987.

Loeb, Robert H., Jr. *Crime and Capital Punishment.* New York: Franklin Watts, 1978.

McCuen, Gary E. and R. A. Baumgart, eds. *Reviving the Death Penalty.* Hudson, Wisconsin: Gary McCuen Publications, Inc., 1985.

Radelet, Michael L., ed. *Facing the Death Penalty, Essays on a Cruel and Unusual Punishment.* Philadelphia: Temple University Press, 1989.

Siegel, Mark A., Carol D. Foster, and Nancy R. Jacobs, eds. *Capital Punishment: Cruel and Unusual?* Wylie, Texas: Information Aids, Inc., 1988.

Smead, Howard. *Blood Justice, The Lynching of Mack Charles Parker.* New York: Oxford University Press, 1986.

Magazine Articles

Boyd, George N. "Capital Punishment: Deserved and Wrong." *The Christian Century,* February 17, 1988, 162-165.

Carroll, Ginny, and Aric Press. "Only Two Weeks to Live." *Newsweek,* August 21, 1989, 62-64.

Dieter, Richard C. "The Death Penalty Dinosaur." *Commonweal,* January 15, 1988, 11-14.

Ellsworth, Phoebe. "Juries on Trial." *Psychology Today,* July, 1985, 44-46.

Goldberg, Steven. "So What if the Death Penalty Deters?" *National Review,* June 30, 1989, 42-44.

Hackett, George et al. "Indiana Killer Italian Martyr." *Newsweek,* September 21, 1987, 37.

Johnson, Robert. "This Man Has Expired." *Commonweal,* January 13, 1989, 9-15.

Kaplan, David A. "Death Rides a Judicial Roller Coaster." *Newsweek,* January 22, 1990, 55.

Kaplan, David A. and Lynda Wright. "Breaking the Death Barrier." *Newsweek,* February 19, 1990, 72-73.

Kaplan, Stanley M. "Death, So Say We All." *Psychology Today,* July, 1985, 48-53.

Koch, Edward I. "Death and Justice." *New Republic*, April 15, 1985, 13-15.

Kramer, Michael. "Cuomo, the Last Holdout." *Time*, April 2, 1990, 20.

Lacayo, Richard. "The Politics of Life and Death." *Time*, April 2, 1990, 18-20.

Newsweek. eds. "Death Row Murderers Could Be Lifesavers." *Newsweek*, January 9, 1989, 49.

Press, Aric and Ginny Carroll. "Execution at an Early Age." *Newsweek*, January 13, 1986, 74.

Press, Aric, Ann McDaniel, Erik Calonius, George Raine, Vern Smith, Andrew Murr, and Daniel Shapiro. "Gridlock on Death Row." *Newsweek*, May 4, 1987, 60-61.

Roberts, Steven and Ted Gest. "A Growing Cry: 'Give Them Death.' " *U.S. News & World Report*, March 26, 1990, 24-25.

Rubenstein, ed. "Crime Pays." *National Review*, June 25, 1990, 15.

Sanders, Alain L. "Bad News for Death Row." *Time Magazine*, July 10, 1989, 48-49.

Smolowe, Jill. "Race and the Death Penalty." *Newsweek*, April 29, 1991, 69.

Stout, David G. "The Lawyers of Death Row." *New York Times Magazine*, February 14, 1988, 46-54.

Van Den Haag, Ernest. "Death and Deterrence." *National Review*, March 14, 1986, 44.

Index

Acknowledgments

The photographs and illustrations in this book are reproduced through the courtesy of: Amnesty International, pp. 6 (top), 21, 30, 66 (top and center); AP/Wide World, pp. 6 (bottom), 9, 24, 28, 39, 42 (bottom), 47, 56 (all), 57 (top), 66 (bottom three), 70, 80 (bottom); the Charlotte Observer (Jeff Siner), pp. 34 (both), 42 (top); Gamma-Liaison, p. 8; Library of Congress, p. 29; Mansell Collection, p. 52 (top and bottom); Office of the Governor of Arkansas, p. 60 (center); UPI/Bettmann, pp. 11 (both), 14, 36, 37, 45 (both), 46, 48, 52 (center), 57 (bottom), 60 (top left and bottom), 72, 76, 80 (top); David Valdez, the White House, p. 60 (top right).

Chart on page 62 adapted from National Center for Policy Analysis data. Graph on page 68 adapted from U.S. Department of Justice, Feredal Bureau of Investigation data. All other charts and graphs are adapted from U.S. Department of Justice, Bureau of Justice Statistics data.